Mandy

FOR GIRLS 1984

CONTENTS

D1357527

£1.95

Look out! There's a bear in the cave!

Do not draw your revolver! I will talk to the bear.

Talk to it? Is she crazy? One swipe from that paw and she'll be dead!

Hold it! Let Valda do things her way.

Do not be selfish, old friend! There is room in this cave for us all to shelter from the storm.

She really is talking to the bear! And it seems to be listening to her!

The bear is going to the back of the cave. We shall be all right just inside if we do not disturb him.

Don't worry, Valda—disturbing grizzlies is something I take mighty good care not to do!

A lot of the wildlife around here is protected. We're looking for a guy reported to be setting illegal traps.

I too am here to help the creatures of the wild against those who try to kill them for selfish gain.

Valda and the two men waited patiently in the cave for several hours. At last—

The snow's stopped. We can be on our way. Thanks for your help, Valda.

I will assist you to dig your helicopter out of the snowfall.

6

The helicopter was soon ready for take-off.

I don't like leaving you out here on your own, Valda. I mean—a girl—dressed like that—in this wilderness—

I am perfectly safe, I assure you. I will call on you sometime at your outpost on Elk River, to show you that I am unharmed.

We abandoned Elk River after our post got flooded out one spring, Valda. Our helicopters operate from Cree Valley now.

I did not know that. It is some years since I was last here. Very well, I will visit you at Cree Valley, sergeant. Goodbye.

Some years since she was last here? What did Valda mean by that? The Elk River post hasn't been used in my time. Yet Valda spoke as if she personally remembered the place!

It's twenty years or more since Elk River was flooded out—before Valda was born! But I've heard old-timers talk of a strange girl who roamed the wilderness way back. Maybe . . .

As Valda continued on her way—

I hear an animal whimpering. Ah! I see—an Arctic hare caught in a cruel trap!

All right, my friend, I'm coming!

I have the trap open. But do not run off yet, hare—I want to see how badly you are hurt.

The leg is not broken. I will rub some snow on the wound, then you can go. The skin will soon heal.

7

"Away with you, hare! Oh, I hear gunshots ahead!"

"A she-wolf and her cubs! You have shot them!"

"A girl—barefoot in the snow! What are you doing here?"

"My name is Valda. And you are the trapper that the police are looking for, I think. I have just released a hare from one of your traps. But I am too late here."

"What? You released a hare? You interfering brat! I just shot these wolves to stop them from raiding my traps!"

"But see! This cub still breathes! Your shot injured it, but did not kill. Now the sun shines, I can use the Crystal of Life to revive it."

"One of the vermin is still alive? Stand aside, girl! I'll finish it off!"

Valda took out the crystal she carried, and held it to the sunlight.

"No! Drop your rifle!"

"Aagh! The light is blinding!"

Your eyes will soon recover. Cool them with snow. Now, little wolf, I will give you back your life. The healing powers of the Crystal of Life pour new strength into you through me.

The cub's on its feet! I can't see any sign of a bullet wound! But I know I shot it!

You did, and to make sure you do not shoot it again—see what has become of your rifle.

Your mother is dead, little one. I will take care of you. But first I must prevent this man from doing more harm. I will bring the police here.

The police? You're not handing me over, girl! I'm clearing off . . . but—but what's the matter with my legs? I can't move!

It is useless to try to move. Now I will signal to the helicopter.

There—there's fire coming from the snow! How can she—?

Something wrong over there! I see a fire! Head for it, Murdoch.

Roger, sarge.

We will go together, little one. I must teach you to live in the wilds. As for you, trapper, I release you from my control. But it is useless for you to run. The police have arrived.

It's Valda again! What's going on, Valda?

This is the man you want, sergeant. I must go. I have work to do.

I see by your teeth that you have finished with milk. We must find you some meat. Here is a fish frozen in the ice of this stream. It will do to start with. I will break it out.

You must learn to work for your food, cub. You must become a hunter. Therefore, chase your dinner!

Your name shall be Silver, for I see silver glints in your fur when the sun strikes it. But I shall not make you a pet. You are a creature of the wild and you must learn to live like other wolves.

Next day—

It is your nature to hunt and kill, so I must help you to gain the skills that will keep you alive. Look, Silver, here are the tracks of a mouse in the snow.

The mouse was too quick for you, Silver. But with every failure you learn a little more.

Valda and Silver stayed together for many months. With Valda's help, the young cub learned to survive in the wilds and to find out just what he could, and couldn't do!

When Spring came—

Here's Valda—she's called to see us, as she promised. Good to know you're well, Valda. Say—look out—there's a half-grown wolf watching us!

POLICE POST CREE VALLEY

That is Silver, the cub I saved from the trapper. He is a little wary of other humans. I cannot stay—he waits for today's hunting lesson.

Look at that! The wolf's walking with Valda like a tame dog! And how can she give it a hunting lesson?

Valda's no ordinary girl—and that'll be no ordinary wolf when she's finished with it!

One evening—

Another wolf howling! You hear the call, Silver. Yes, you have learned your skills well and you are ready to go now. I am sorry we must part, but in a life like mine there are many farewells.

It is time for you to join your own kind, Silver. That is where you belong. Goodbye, my friend. May fortune smile on you.

Those were happy months while I was Silver's teacher. I shall miss him. But it was right for him to go. I will not leave yet, however. I will stay for the winter's first snows, to make sure that I have been successful in teaching Silver how to survive.

When winter closed in again—

Tracks left by a pack of wolves! And Silver is with them. His prints are distinctive, and I recognise them. He has been accepted by his own kind, and all is well. Now I can move on.

Something is wrong—not with the wolves, but there is danger somewhere. I feel it.

My feeling of uneasiness is stronger here. Yes, that truck. It is being driven much too fast!

It has gone off the road!

The driver has been flung out. And the snow on the slope above is ready to fall! The crash has disturbed it.

It is the trapper who shot Silver's mother!

Valda! Help me! My leg's trapped! I think it's broken!

Try to slide out as I take the weight.

I can feel the pressure lifting! My stars, you're moving the truck off me! But that's impossible!

I'm clear! Look out, the snow's moving! There's an avalanche starting!

Shelter by the truck—quickly!

Aah!

Valda!

At last the rush of snow ceased.

Valda! Where are you? Valda, I'm trapped in the snow! Help me!

I cannot reach you!

Valda, do something! You know my leg is broken! What's the matter with you? You look tired and old, all of a sudden!

I have no strength left. Now we both know what it feels like to be trapped!

And I have lost the Crystal of Life! The cord of my pouch snapped when the avalanche struck, and the snow carried the pouch away. Lifting the truck drained my strength, and I am helpless to renew it.

Suddenly—

A wolf! We'll be torn to pieces!

No! It's Silver! He sensed my danger. He has come to help!

He's digging in the snow!

He's found something!

My good friend, Silver, brings the pouch to me.

It—it's incredible!

The Crystal of Life renews me! Now I can free myself.

Aah! It's that crystal thing again.

14

Galloping THROUGH THE AGES

ABOUT HORSES

Sixty million years ago, a tiny creature, less than a foot high, ran across the plains of the earth. This little animal, HYRACOTHERIUM, was the ancestor of today's horse. He had four toes on his front feet, and three on his hind feet, and is more commonly known as EOHIPPUS, which means, in Greek, the "DAWN HORSE"

Four types of horse have sprung from this "DAWN HORSE"—in Europe, a heavy, draught type horse; in Asia the TARPAN and PRZEVALSKI'S HORSE; and in Africa the EQUUS AGILIS. It was this last horse, ancestor of all today's "light" breeds, that the Arabs and Egyptians used.

In Northern Europe, the heavy horse carried armoured knights. Then, later, horses were used for transport, pulling carriages and carts.

Even today, horses are still useful, although mostly for pleasure—with pony trekking now a very popular pastime.

CONTINUED ON PAGE 41.

Dilly The Daily

DILLY worked as a daily to make some extra pocket money during the school holidays. She had been asked to clean a house once a week for a couple who were abroad—

Looks like this is going to take a while—lucky it's only once a week!

This is the kitchen in here—well, I'd better get started.

Two weeks later, on her third visit—

I hear voices! But there can't be anyone in the house . . . can there?

If we make the raid at two a.m., the security guard will be having his break.

Yeah—we should get a big haul from this.

They're planning a robbery! I'll have to get the police. I can't phone from here, though—they might hear me!

I only hope they come before the thieves leave.

Thank goodness—there's a phone box at the end of the street here.

Yes . . . a robbery . . . What? Oh—Twenty Elmgrove Road. Come quickly. Yes, I'll be there. I'll wait outside.

Soon—

Thank goodness they've arrived! I think the thieves are still in there.

19

I'm really sorry. You see, I didn't know that you'd come back, and . . .

Don't apologise. You did the right thing, so don't worry. Now, how about a cup of tea?

Later—

And you're actors? It must be great fun. I've always fancied acting myself.

Paul, are you thinking what *I'M* thinking?

I certainly am. What a good idea.

What is it? What's a good idea?

A few days later—

Imagine—me acting—and all because I called the police!

Well, the girl who was playing the cleaner fell ill, so . . . Besides, the part is ideal for you. You've only got a small part to play—but it'll suit you . . .

. . . *SHE'S* the one who informs the police!

THE END

A BIT, DAMP

"**OH, it's you!**" I said as I opened the door and saw my brother's friend, James, standing there. "**Ken's out, if you want him.**"

"**No, I don't want to see Ken. It was you, Nikki. I wanted to ask if y-y-y . . .**" James began to stammer, and I heard a muffled giggle from behind the laurel bush by the gate.

"**If I'd what?**" I prompted, with an exasperated sigh. Really, James Potter was the absolute end. Thin and scrawny looking, untidy and so awkward that he was always falling over his own feet, which seemed too big for the rest of him.

I was in no mood to be patient. Hadn't I, that very afternoon, seen Lewis Atkins go by with my best friend, Una? Lewis Atkins, the boy every girl in our year thought was really great.

Ever since then, I'd been moping in my room, because I'd honestly thought he liked me, after last night at the disco. Now, to be disturbed from my good mope by James Potter was a bit much.

"If you—you—." He shifted uneasily from foot to foot. "Er . . . If you—" There was a snort of laughter from the bushes, and I saw two boys run away.

"Oh, well, never mind," said James, turning a peculiar crimson colour, as he turned to go down the path. Something about his hunched, dejected looking shoulders made me feel sympathetic.

"James! Come back here, a minute. They dared you, didn't they?"

"Sort of," he turned and nodded. "They said I was too wet to ask a girl to go out with me, and we were just passing your gate, so I thought, well, you're Ken's sister, and so I—oh, well, it doesn't matter."

He was just about to take off again, so I had to get my important question in pretty quickly!

"One of them was Lewis Atkins' brother, wasn't he?" He nodded again. I smiled my sweetest smile. "Right. I'd like to come out with you, James. Now—if you like. I'll get my jacket."

"Really, Nikki?" He looked as if he couldn't believe his luck. "That'll be smashing. Get your bike, and perhaps we could go down to the coast."

He had his own bike propped up against the wall outside, and as we set off down the road, I pretended not to see young Atkins and his friend, watching us open-mouthed from the corner. And I knew that he was bound to tell Lewis. Then he'd know that I didn't have to sit around waiting for HIM!

I laughed to show how light-hearted I was, though a small voice inside warned me that with James Potter—well, I'd be a laughing stock!

Too late now, though. I was committed to an afternoon with boring James!

"There's a high tide this afternoon," James mentioned, as we cycled along the quiet lanes. "I thought we could go down to Gannet Bay and watch the waves—should be spectacular, especially with this wind!"

Wind, he called it. After we'd been cycling for several miles, it was more like a force-ten gale, and it was blowing right into our faces! It became difficult even to talk—the words were snatched away as soon as I opened my mouth. But it was exhilarating, and I found myself laughing as we struggled on. Soon we turned off the road and into a rutted lane that twisted down-hill between high hedges. James was worried about my bike on the bumpy track, and I had to keep reassuring him that I was okay.

And then we were at the bottom, looking past a group of derelict cottages to an old, weed-grown quay, partly fallen away, and the remains of a battered breakwater running seawards until it stopped in a jumble of piled stones.

"This used to be a busy little fishing place," said James. "Until a bad storm hit it, about twelve years ago. The sea washed away the boats, broke right over the quay and actually smashed two of the old houses. Nobody's lived here since."

"Then what's that?" I asked, pointing.

Further along, and standing on its own, was a cottage that seemed fairly intact, and there was a wisp of smoke coming out of the chimney.

"I didn't realise anyone was left here," said James, looking puzzled. "Must be a tramp, I should think. Anyway, put your bike here." So I propped my bicycle beside his, against the wall of the nearest tumbledown cottage. Then we picked our way among scattered stones to the quay.

"Don't go too near the edge," cautioned James. "It isn't very safe, and might crumble beneath you." He said it would be spectacular, and it certainly was. The tide was still some way out, beyond a strip of shingle and pebbles, but enormous waves were breaking over the pile of massive stones that marked the end of the breakwater. As we sat on a huge block of concrete, James produced some chocolate, and we munched away companionably, huddled up against the wind,

and feeling the blown spray on our faces.

I realised I was enjoying myself. James might be a bit wet, but he knew a lot about the history of the place, and made it really interesting. His stammer had disappeared, now that he was no longer nervous, and he was just telling me about the night, all those years ago, when three people had been drowned in the great waves that smashed over their house, when, right on cue, a real wave crashed up against the quay and drenched us.

We retreated very quickly, a few yards, and watched in awe as one after another, the great breakers came sweeping in to the little bay—some were washing right over the quay itself! It was very exciting, but then it got scary too, as we saw the huge piece of concrete, on which we had been sitting, picked up, tossed away, and swept over the quayside as though it had been a pebble.

"Time we were off," said James, for now every wave was thundering over the quay, breaking it into crashing slabs, which fell down, on to the shingle.

"That was marvellous," I said as we rushed back to the shelter of the wall, where we had left the bikes. "But it must have been terrifying for those folk who lived here on the night of the great storm."

"It isn't even high tide yet," said James, shouting above the noise of the wind. "We'll retreat up the hill a bit, and watch from there."

It was when we had pushed our bikes a safe distance up the hill that we remembered.

"The tramp!" we both said together. At that moment, a

bigger wave than ever came towering in over the quay, broke, and then seethed forward until water lapped right up to the wall of one of the derelict cottages.

"I'll have to go down," said James. "You stay here."

"No fear, I'm coming too," I said, as I threw my bike into the hedge and ran back down the slope with James.

A tangle of bramble hedge made it impossible to go through the back gardens of the cottages; the only way to the one with the smoking chimney was along the quay itself.

"Come on!" said James, grabbing my hand as a wave broke, and receded. Then we splashed through ankle-deep water, and just made it before the next wave broke.

The cottage we were aiming for stood back a little, so that, as yet, no water had

reached it.

"I'm going in," said James, when our knocking at the door received no answer. Lifting the latch, he pushed open the door and stepped inside, and I followed.

I don't know what I expected, but certainly not the bright cheerful room in which we stood. A fire of driftwood burned in the old-fashioned grate; wild flowers were in a jug on the table, and a grandfather clock tocked slowly in the corner. I took all this in within seconds, and then saw the bed along one wall.

Clutching a patchwork quilt up to her chin, a white-haired old lady gazed at us in terror.

"It's all right," said James gently, going across to her. She shrank back against the pillow.

"I've nothing for you," she said in a quavery voice. "There's my pension in that purse; take it, and leave me alone."

I went across then, and knelt by the bed. I smiled, and she seemed reassured.

"We haven't come to hurt you," I said. "It's just that the storm is getting worse, and the sea is right up over the quay. We've come to help you to safety."

"No, no!" she said in a stronger voice. "They couldn't shift me last time, and I'm not shifting now. Anyway, I've hurt my leg, that's why I'm in bed. Can't walk more than a step or two."

A crash outside made James and me run to the window. A huge wave had smashed against the empty cottage next door, and we watched as the wall disappeared in a boiling froth of water. It was terrifying.

"We've got to get her out," said James, in a whisper. "This is worse than twelve

23

years ago, because the sea defences have never been repaired.''

''But she's so old,'' I whispered back. ''And she can't walk. We'd never carry her through this!''

''It would kill her,'' he whispered even more softly. ''You are going to get help. I'll stay here with her until someone comes.'' He sounded calm, but there was just a tremor in his voice as he added, ''Make it as quick as you can, won't you, Nikki?''

I didn't stop to argue. I opened the door, letting in the howling gale, and, as he struggled to shut it behind me, I heard him speak cheerfully to the old woman.

''I'll just make us a cup of tea, eh, Gran?'' he said, and then I was alone, facing that return journey along the quay, with waves regularly breaking right across it.

I was frightened to death, but I knew it took more courage to stay in that tiny room behind me, not knowing how long the old walls would resist the tide. I watched one wave, larger than the rest, break and go back, and then I ran.

I nearly made it, but when I had only yards to go, I slipped on the wet cobbles, and went sprawling. I looked up, to see a mountain of water towering over me. Then suddenly, I saw right by my hand, a metal post, all that remained of a garden gate. I threw both arms around it, and hung on. The wall of water broke over me, and then I felt the terrible suction as it tried to drag me back with it. How I managed to hold on I shall never know, but desperation gave me strength.

Gasping, I lay there, battered and numb, but thank goodness, I still retained enough sense to realise my danger. So, I scrambled to my feet, and hurled myself the last few yards, and this time I made it.

I was safe around the corner of the cottage before the next breaker came in. No time to stand and try to get my breath back. With water dripping from my clothes I started to run up the hill; snatched up my bike and pushed it up that steep lane.

At the top, I wondered which way to go, desperately trying to remember if we had passed a phone box on our way. Then I remembered passing a farm. I jumped on the saddle, and, pedalling frantically, fairly flew along the road, with gusts of wind threatening to push me over sideways.

The farm was just where I remembered it, and I raced up to the door, and hammered on it. As soon as I told the farmer, he had his wife send for an ambulance. Then he collected his two sons, and I jumped up

into the farm truck with them, hanging on like grim death as we hurtled back the way I had come.

"I thought they'd moved the old lady out, but she must have given them the slip. Always strong-willed, was Granny Munro!" The farmer spoke with what sounded rather like admiration.

I kept on thinking of James; feeble James who had calmly taken charge of the situation, and stayed in great danger without a second thought. I hoped desperately that he was all right.

Halfway down the steep lane, the farmer stopped and one of his sons opened a field gate.

"Can't risk the old quay," said the farmer, trying to inch carefully down the slope. Our progress seemed so slow, but I knew haste would be dangerous.

Suddenly, we were there, looking down upon the back of the old lady's cottage, through a gap in a thick hedge. But my heart gave a lurch and I cried out.

The sea had completely surrounded the little house, and with each wave that crashed against the front wall, two great tongues of water

raced to join up behind the cottage.

And then I saw a figure at an upstairs window. It was James.

"Hi, there!" he said, calmly. "Nice to see you."

The three men ran down the bank and splashed into waist-deep water, while I stayed, watching and shivering.

"It wasn't too nice downstairs," said James. "So Gran and I thought it would be better up here."

That was all he said, but I could imagine the struggles he must have had, getting her up those narrow stairs.

"All right, lad," said the farmer, as another huge wave hit the cottage. One of his sons climbed on his shoulders, gripped the edge of the window sill and heaved himself through. A surge of water rose around the chests of the other two men. We waited. Then there was a pair of strong arms, handing out a blanket-wrapped bundle to waiting hands below. The farmer took the bundle as if it weighed nothing, and splashed back to the bank where I stood. The outraged face of the little old lady peered out from the blankets.

"Perfectly all right," she was saying indignantly, "no need to go shifting a body like this!"

Even as she spoke, the old cottage gave up the struggle. The next wave proved too much for the crumbling walls. With a groaning crash they gave way at last, and the sea covered the remains of the old lady's home.

Just in time, James and the farmer's son jumped from the window, and I watched with my hands over my mouth as three figures struggled in the seething water. And then they were clambering up the bank, to stand dripping beside us.

"Ah, well, it wasn't too good for my rheumatics," Granny Munro announced philosophically, as the truck thundered back across the fields.

"Too damp down there," she added, as we left her in the ambulance in the lane.

James and I looked at each other, both soaked to the skin and with hair in rats' tails, and started to laugh.

"Just a bit damp," we agreed.

Damp, James may have been, but nobody is ever again going to tell me that he's wet!

25

IN 1320, Miranda Pickard was on her way to join her father in the far corners of Russia, where he had gone to live, after hearing tales of a land fabulously rich in silks and precious stones.

It has been many months since I've seen my father, but soon we shall meet again, and I shall begin my new life in a new country.

The PRINCESS and the SLAVE

Just then—

Pirates!

Hurry, men—to battle stations! Prepare to fight.

Seize the girl!

Will they kill us all? Am I never to see my dear father again?

We shall soon be landing in Tartar country, where you will be sold to work as a slave to some wealthy household!

I must be strong! Father said the Tartars are cruel, hard people, but I must not show my fear of them!

Once on land, Miranda was taken to a market place—

This man must be looking for a slave. But he looks so unkind, I fear he would not be a good master. Oh, how I wish I were safely with my father.

I'll take this one. Her golden hair and fair skin are a novelty. It may please Princess Sula to have this strange creature as her servant!

I am to belong to a princess. Perhaps I will be lucky—life with a princess should not be too hard. I hope . . .

Your new slave, Princess. Her name is Miranda.

She looks frail, but perhaps she will do.

Princess Sula looks haughty and aloof. Yet there is a sadness about her, as if something is troubling her.

To test you, slave, I want you to fill my water carrier—Sungan will show you how. Spill even a drop, and you shall be punished severely!

Very well, Princess.

Sungan is not watching me. Perhaps this is my chance to escape.

The slave is escaping.

He's seen me!

That was a stupid thing to do, slave. Now you shall be punished. I will take you back to the princess—she will wish to deal with you herself.

There is only one punishment for slaves who try to escape—the wooden collar. See to it, Sungan.

Yes, Princess.

The wooden collar? What is that?

A large wooden collar was placed round Miranda's neck and locked securely—

It is heavy and horrible. I shall never be able to run away wearing this. I am a prisoner—for ever!

Next day, Miranda was summoned by Princess Sula—

We are to set out on a long journey, and you must prepare my things. We are travelling to the court of the Great Khan. I am to marry his son, whom I have never seen.

You are to marry a man you have never seen? But that's horrible.

I agree, Miranda, but what can I do? The marriage has been arranged by my father and the Great Khan, in order to keep peace between our two peoples. I cannot go against my father's wishes.

Leave me now—you have work to do! We leave at dawn tomorrow.

Yes, Princess.

Princess Sula is not as brave as she seems. I feel sorry for her, in spite of what she has done to me.

At dawn the next day—

You shall behave yourself on this journey, slave, and work hard. If not, I may no longer have any use for you once we reach our destination.

Yes, Princess.

I am no longer afraid of the princess and her threats, now I know she has weaknesses too.

That night, after the party had made camp—

Sula—look out!

28

Ah—it's bitten me!

I know what to do.

You are sucking the poison from the bite.

You saved my life. Thank you!

I only did it because a slave's no good to me dead.

Poor Sula has never been allowed to show her true feelings. It would not be fitting for a princess to show friendship to a slave. Even though I'm sure she needs a friend.

The next day, the sun beat strongly on the party—

I never thought this country could be so dry and hot. I hope we reach a water hole soon, I don't think we've much left.

Fetch me water, slave. I'm thirsty.

But, Princess, there is not much left.

But Sula insisted.

Now there is no water for anyone else. But there is supposed to be a water hole near here—if it hasn't dried up, of course.

They seemed to be in luck—

A water hole!

Water—at last!

A water hole . . . but it's almost empty! And the water's a strange colour. But in this strange country, nothing surprises me.

Bring me water, slave. I'm thirsty.

We all are, but *WE* can only take a small sip, so we can have enough for the rest of the journey.

— Sula can drink her fill, but we are only allowed a small sip to try to quench our thirst!

That night—

Sula's gone—but where to? Oh . . . my head, I feel so weak . . . I suspected there was something wrong with that water, and I'm right!

There she is. Perhaps she has a fever from the water . . . after all, she drank more than anyone else, so it will affect her more. I must go after her!

Ha—the great warrior! I shall soon show you who is the greatest! Prepare to fight.

She is attacking a harmless monument of some kind! I must stop her before she harms herself—or anyone else. I have a length of rope attached to my saddle . . . I wonder . . .

See! She is harming the princess!

She must be punished!

I must explain I was only trying to save the princess—not harming her.

But—

No one must touch the princess in such a manner. You *MUST* die—it is the law!

No—stop! Give me the sword!

So I am to die at her hand. I thought Sula was my friend—but it seems she cares nothing for me.

But—

I know what you tried to do, and I thank you. You are free.

Thank you, Princess Sula. I am grateful.

Next day—

Look, Princess. That tall building must be the palace of the Great Khan.

I fear so, Miranda. I can only pray that the man I am to marry will be kind. Guards— we must go straight to the palace.

So you are Sula. My son shall be here shortly. I trust your journey went well.

Yes, thank you, Great Khan.

Ah, my son! This is your bride. Is she not beautiful?

The young Khan looks kind—and he's handsome too! I am happy for Sula— she will have a good life. If only I knew what was to become of me . . .

Ah, my ambassador has come to welcome our guests.

Father, Father!

Miranda—I've found you!

This is wonderful—we have had two happy events in one day! You shall both be honoured guests at my son's wedding.

And so—

An adventure that began so badly has ended happily. No longer am I the girl with the wooden collar!

Mandy

The Gift

GAYE SMALL was a thirteen-year-old girl, who had up till now led a pretty normal sort of life—

'Night, Mum.

Goodnight, dear—but isn't it awfully early for you to go to bed? After all, it *IS* the holidays.

She needs her beauty sleep, Mum!

If I wasn't so tired, Paul, I'd come over and thump you!

Sweet dreams, love.

But that night, Gaye's dreams were strange ones—

Next morning—

What a peculiar dream! I read that dreams have some bearing on reality—but not in this case. The only dog we had was a guide dog we looked after for a year.

Oh, well, I don't suppose it'll ever be explained—dreams never are.

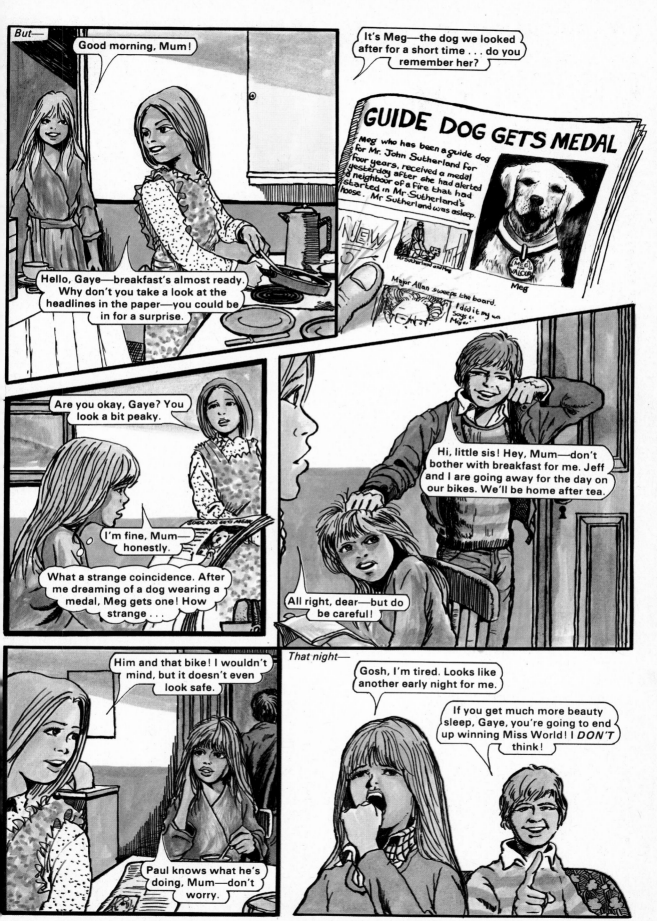

Another dream—but it's impossible. Paul could never win a race on *HIS* old wreck!

It more often than not doesn't even go!

Later—

Broken down again, Paul?

'Fraid so—hey—while you're here you can help me take Dad's tool box out of the garage.

Suddenly—

Oh, no—my bike! It'll be ruined!

I'm terribly sorry. I don't know what I was thinking about. I was just reversing into your drive, and . . . Look, let me just compensate you now. It'll save a lot of bother with insurance and such like . . .

Well, if you think that's best.

But my bike isn't worth anything like that much!

That's okay, son! Keep it to compensate you for the inconvenience!

38

You see, lass, you're seeing into the future—although the message of the dream is often difficult to understand at the time. But no one can change the future—so you mustn't try. It can only cause trouble.

So there's nothing I can do?

No—but don't let it worry you. Plenty people have The Gift—nothing need come of it. You'll learn to live with it and not let it frighten you. Now—how about a nice cup of tea?

That night—

I don't want to go to sleep. I don't want to dream. Oh, I don't want to go to sleep . . .

Next morning—

What an awful night. I didn't get a wink of sleep! Still, it meant I didn't have any dreams!

But, that afternoon—

I'm so tired . . . it's no use, I HAVE to sleep . . . I HAVE to.

Soon Gaye was dreaming again—

GAYE SMALL
R.I.P.

1970

HORSES ON SHOW

Among the most impressive horses in the world are the grey Lippizaner stallions of the Spanish Riding School in Vienna.

Another place where performing horses can be seen, is the circus. Here the variety is vast, from the comical clown's pony to the Western act.

The "giants" of the horse-world—Shires, Clydesdales, Percherons, Rhenish, Suffolk Punches, and many others, can be seen at the numerous Agricultural Shows held up and down the country.

Other types of horse include hunters, racers, show-jumpers and gymkhana ponies.

Finally, there are the horses of the Household Cavalry, often seen on state occasions and on guard duty.

CONTINUED ON PAGE 81.

TONI GRANT loved Pop music. She thought it was out of this world.

Blue Moon Pink Stars

What a night! There's been thunder and lightning for ages! I'm glad I'm not going to the disco till later.

That was a loud clap of thunder— at least I *THINK* it was . . . maybe our oak tree's fallen down! I'd better take a look.

But Toni wasn't dreaming!

The moon . . . it can't be, it's blue! And the stars are *PINK!* That's impossible. I must be dreaming . . .

Mum . . . Dad . . . it's the moon! It's blue!

What *ARE* you talking about, Toni? It's always been blue—now sit down and have your breakfast!

At the disco—

Could you play this request, please?

The record plays from the middle outwards—and nobody's dancing—they're just all sitting about. I don't understand.

Em, why don't we dance, Lee? This is a good record.

Dance? Ha! Ha! Where do you think you are, Toni? You know dancing is only allowed in Public Libraries and Museums!

That night—

Everybody's doing and saying things that are so strange, so different. Yet the town looks as it always did, and the people look like the people I've known all my life. There's school tomorrow, too, although I thought it was Sunday—what on earth is it going to be like?

Now, children—we'll start at page one hundred, and finish at ninety. Toni—you start reading, please.

But, Miss, I . . .

No wonder you don't know what you're doing—you're holding the book upside down.

UPSIDE DOWN? But it's the right way up, at least, it always was before!

By lunchtime, Toni was thoroughly mixed up.

I've been kept in—because I said Shakespeare wrote ' Romeo and Juliet! The teacher said I was being cheeky! Oh, I wish I could go home, no matter how mixed up it is there!

Hello. Toni, isn't it? I'm Jon. I just thought I'd keep you company. Is everything okay?

Everything's NOT okay— that's the trouble! Oh, I have to tell someone.

When Toni had finished—

You do believe me, don't you? You don't believe I'm imagining things, do you?

No. I've read a lot of books about things like this—and I believe you CAN be transported to ' another world '. Our Toni's probably as confused as you are.

OUR Toni! Maybe that's it! Maybe I've changed places with another girl called Toni from a different world of some sort! Oh, this is all IMPOSSIBLE!

Classes are finished now. Look, I'll call for you after breakfast this evening—you can take me for a coffee if you like!

Oh well, at least I've got a friend, anyway. I hope he can help me! I don't know how I got into this mess—and I certainly don't know how I'm going to get out of it!

Back at Toni's home—

Hello, dear. Dad's working early tonight, so we'll just have our meal now. It's your favourite—treacle tart followed by liver and potatoes.

I HATE liver and I can't STAND treacle tart—I suppose I should have known it would be my "favourite".

Finished—thank goodness!

I'll wash up, Mum.

How DARE you speak to me like that! Go to your room at once! You've been acting VERY strangely lately, Toni. Perhaps you're not feeling quite right—but I will NOT stand for insolence.

What did I say this time? Oh, I give up!

There's a storm brewing—if that's allowed in this crazy world!

Music's the same here anyway, except for the records being played backwards. I wonder if I'll ever get used to it?

Suddenly a loud clap of thunder startled Toni.

Goodness, it's got quite dark outside, and the moon . . .

. . . it's normal! And the stars are back to normal, too!

Mum—you . . . you're *WASHING-UP!*

Well, that's what usually happens after tea, dear. There's the doorbell. Will you answer it, please?

Jon—you look worried! What's wrong?

Er, well, I know this is going to sound pretty silly, Toni, but the truth is that since that last lot of thunder . . . well . . . it's the moon and stars, actually . . . er, well, they seem to me to have turned *YELLOW!*

THE END

WHAT'S COOKING?
(or how to feed a fisherman)

There you are casually walking past the river bank (where you KNOW he'll be fishing), when you see him emerge from the water soaked to the skin. Yes, you're right—he's fallen in. This is where you immediately invite him home to dry out and have a meal (don't worry if you can't cook; read on and you'll be able to). Whatever else you do, DON'T ask him how many fish he's caught—he probably hasn't caught any!

STUFFED BAKED POTATOES

2 potatoes
½ oz. (12 g.) grated cheese
Little butter
Milk
Seasoning

Oven—400 deg. F., 200 deg. C., Gas mark 6, for 1 hour.

Clean potatoes thoroughly and brush skins with melted butter.

Cut round top of potatoes to make a lid, but don't cut all the way through.

Place on baking tray and bake.

Take lids off and scoop out potatoes, trying not to split skin.

Mash potatoes with cheese, butter, milk and seasoning.

Put mixture back in potatoes, sprinkle with cheese, and return to oven till hot.

APPLE DUMPLINGS
Shortcrust Pastry

4 oz. (100 g.) plain flour
2 oz. (50 g.) fat
½ oz. (12 g.) sugar
Water to mix

2 large apples
1 oz. (25 g.) brown sugar
Cinnamon

Oven—400 deg. F., 200 deg. C., Gas mark 6, for 30 mins.

Rub together fat and flour till it looks like breadcrumbs. Add sugar and mix.

Add water a little at a time, and mix in to make soft dough.

Peel and core apples, and fill centre with the brown sugar and cinnamon to taste.

Divide pastry in two, then roll out pieces into rounds.

Wrap pastry round apples, sealing with water.

Place on greased baking sheet, brush with milk and sprinkle over some castor sugar. Bake.

Serve hot with cream.

Put in the Apple Dumplings when the potatoes have been in 45 minutes—that way they'll be ready when you want them.

After he's eaten he SHOULD be a lot more cheerful (depending on your cooking)! You'll note that none of our recipes include fish—you can guess why! It would also be wise not to mention fish, fishing or water. This is called tact.

After all this he should ask you out. If he does—good, your effort hasn't been wasted. If he DOESN'T, DON'T threaten to throw him back where you found him, he isn't even worth that. Just smile sweetly, and start looking around for someone else to practise your new found culinary skills on!

The SEARCH

THERE was no hint of the disaster to come as Barbara looked over the fence towards the riding stables. The scene, in fact, was much as it usually was. Some horses were stabled, dozing in the sun, their heads nodding over the half-doors, others were being groomed in the yard, alert, ears pricked and coats gleaming. She was careful to keep out of sight, knowing the Head Groom, Wally Jenkins, would soon yell at her to be off if he caught sight of her.

Barbara loved ponies and horses, and when her family moved and she found the new house was near a riding school, she couldn't believe her luck. At first, she had gone there with confidence, offering to help, but since her encounter with Mr Jenkins, she hadn't tried again.

"What are you hanging around for?" he'd snapped at her. "There's enough to do without having to trip over kids all day!"

"That's just it," said Barbara, eagerly. "I'd like to help, if you'll let me."

The man just laughed in her face.

"You!" he sneered. "What could a little kid like you do? We need real help—not just silly kids who don't know one end of a horse from another. Buzz off!" he shouted at her. "And don't come bothering me again."

After that, Barbara kept her distance, but all the same, couldn't resist watching without being seen. And sometimes when the animals were grazing, she'd slip into the field and talk to them.

Barbara had a particular favourite, a small bay pony called Dandy. Dandy was never used for lessons at the Riding School, and Barbara felt sorry for the pony, who she felt sure, must get bored.

Barbara managed to get to know some of the other people who worked at the stables, and found them all much friendlier than Mr Jenkins. Susan was one of the girls who gave lessons, and she told Barbara that Mr Jenkins was often bad-tempered.

"Except with the horses," she said, "He seems to like *THEM* all right. And he knows a lot about them too. I expect that's why they keep him on, because he's so good at his job."

"But not so good with people?" Barbara asked.

" You can say that again!" Susan laughed.

That evening, while Barbara was doing her homework, her younger brother burst in.

" Hey! Know what?" he babbled excitedly. " There's a fire at the stables! Smoke and flames everywhere! And there's fire engines, and . . ."

Barbara didn't wait to hear any more. She ran up the lane as fast as she could towards the stables.

A scene of utter confusion confronted her. Black smoke swirled everywhere, and beyond the fire engines she could see the dull red glow of one gutted stable, and another with the forked flames still leaping. Shouting people jostled all round her, and there was an acrid, choking smell.

" The horses and ponies! Where are they?" Barbara gasped tearfully at the people around her—but nobody answered. Then she saw Susan, her face streaked with dirt, running towards the gate.

" Susan! Where are they?" Barbara called.

Susan saw her, and understood at once.

" We managed to get them all out!" she gasped as she ran, " and they've all bolted! We're going to try and catch them now."

Barbara ran at her side, heart pounding.

" How did it happen?" she asked, " What started it?"

" I don't know," answered Susan, her dark hair bouncing on her back. " We'll find out later. The important thing now is to round up the ponies."

They ran with the others from the stables to the fields which were used by the horses for grazing in the summer, and at the bottom of the second field, found them all bunched together, trembling and hot. Mr Jenkins forgot to be cross, in his relief at finding them. He checked each animal individually, then barked out orders to his staff.

" See to it! Don't skimp any of it." He turned to Susan. " I see you've got that kid with you," he said. " Well, maybe she'll be useful for once. There's one pony missing. While the others are busy here, we'll have to look for him. It's Dandy."

" Dandy?" said Susan. " He's a nervous pony at the best of times. In his terror, he could have bolted anywhere!"

" I know that, girl!" snapped Mr Jenkins. " Come on, we're wasting time. You two search the surrounding fields on foot. I'll go back for the truck and look in the lanes."

So Susan and Barbara tramped through the fields, calling Dandy's name, but to no

avail. It was getting late, and the light was beginning to fade, so Barbara knew she would have to go back.

" We'll both go back," Susan said, her voice taut with worry. " I don't know what Mr Jenkins will do if Dandy isn't found safe. Dandy belongs to him, you know, and for some reason he won't let anybody ever ride him."

" Maybe we'll find he's there when we get back," suggested Barbara hopefully.

But he wasn't. Nobody at the stables had seen him at all. The fire was out by then, and all that remained of the stables was a blackened, smoking ruin. All the horses were safe, fed and soothed in the field. All except

Dandy. Sadly, Barbara went home, impatient for the morning.

There was no school the next day, as it was Saturday, but Barbara was up early, eager to check at the stables for any news. The only person that seemed to be about was one of the stable lads. She asked about Dandy.

" Oh yes," he said. " They found Dandy all right. Over in the big wood. But he won't let anyone near him. Scared out of his wits, he is!"

She ran home for her bike, and pedalled furiously along the lanes to the wood. Leaving the bike in the hedge, she followed the paths, stopping every now and then to listen. At last, she heard low voices, and as she followed their direction, she saw that Mr Jenkins, Susan and a stable lad were all standing in a clearing. They had halters, and were looking towards the hedge that formed the boundary at that part of the wood. There Dandy trembled, his scorched coat darkened by sweat as well as fire.

"Dandy," called Barbara softly.

The pony's head turned to look at her.

"He won't let us near him," Susan said. "The poor thing is still terrified after last night."

"The kid might stand a chance," Mr Jenkins said suddenly. "She's smaller you see, and Dandy was used to being handled by . . . by somebody small, like her. He might trust her."

Barbara walked towards Dandy. She knew a sudden movement would make him uneasy, so she went a few yards past him, repeating the pony's name quietly and calmly, and waited. Dandy's ears pricked forward.

"That's it," she said encouragingly. "Good boy. Come on then."

"What's this then, boy?" said Barbara, remembering the apple she had in her pocket. She held it out, and slowly Dandy moved nearer, step by step. Barbara held her breath. Would he just snatch it and wheel away again? Praying he wouldn't, she felt the pony's warm breath on her outstretched palm, and quickly she stroked his neck with her other hand.

"Good boy!" she praised him, and went on talking to him, not daring to try and hold him until he was calm. The others watched her, and then at last when Dandy was standing quietly, Barbara slipped an arm right round his neck, and knew the battle was over.

Mr Jenkins slid the halter gently on the now quiet animal.

"You had a nasty fright, didn't you, old boy?" he said. "Never mind. You'll be fine now. It's all over. We'll take you home now, back to your old friends. You'll stay with him too, won't you—er—er . . ?"

"Her name's Barbara," Susan told him. "She's very good with horses."

"I can see that," said Mr Jenkins. "Better than I gave her credit for. I doubt if many people could have dealt with Dandy the way she did. I'm sorry I was so short with you before, Barbara."

Susan looked astonished. She'd never known Mr Jenkins apologise to anyone before. She was even more surprised when Mr Jenkins went on to ask Barbara if she was still interested in helping at the stables sometimes.

"There's this old fellow for a start," he said. "He gets a bit lonely, I know. Maybe you'd like to ride him and groom him now and again?"

Later, when Barbara was spilling the whole story out to her parents, her father suddenly interrupted.

"Funny chap, that Wally Jenkins," he said. "But I heard something today about him that maybe explains his manner. He had a real tragedy a couple of years ago, and lost his wife and children in a car smash. It happened before he came here, so not many people know about it."

"I suppose Dandy belonged to his children?" Barbara asked.

"To the little girl, I gather," her father said. "She was only twelve when she was killed."

"So that's what he meant when he said Dandy was used to someone smaller," said Barbara. "I understand now. Poor man, I didn't know."

"I daresay he'll mellow in time," said her Dad, "but it can take a long time to get over a terrible shock like that."

Like Dandy, Barbara thought. It'll take time for him too. Well, maybe I can do some good for both of them, with patience. Mr Jenkins and Dandy together, they both trust me now, and that's what they both need—someone to trust.

The Letter

MELANIE EDWARDS had recently moved to a new town—

I suppose I ought to start off to school. Oh, I wish I didn't have to go. It's so big and noisy—not like my old school.

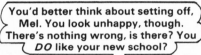

You'd better think about setting off, Mel. You look unhappy, though. There's nothing wrong, is there? You *DO* like your new school?

Of course I do. And you're right, I'd better make a move.

I can't tell Mum and Dad how unhappy I am—they've been looking forward to moving here for ages. Besides, things *MAY* get better. After all, I haven't been here that long, really.

Look at that dress, isn't it awful?

I'd rather wear school uniform than that!

I wish I had friends to joke with. Never mind it's cookery first. I'll enjoy that.

It took me ages to find the cookery room. But I've made it—just. I don't think I'll ever find my way about here.

Now girls, if you'll pair up and take a bench each.

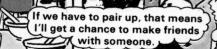

If we have to pair up, that means I'll get a chance to make friends with someone.

But—

Oh . . . I suppose you'll have to work on your own. There's a spare unit at the back there.

Yes, Miss.

It looks like I'll have to work alone, after all.

Why did we have to move house? Why did Dad have to get promoted? I hate it here! I *HATE* it!

At lunch—

Oh good. There's a spare seat with those girls from my class. I may be able to get talking to them.

I hope they're friendly. I hate talking to people I don't know, but I'll have to pluck up courage and make the effort.

Hi, Karen.

Hi. Hey, guess what happened in Maths today . . .

There's no room for me there. They don't want me . . .

...*NO ONE* wants me—I'll *NEVER* make any friends.

After lunch—

There's no address on it, only a name—Abbie Williams. I don't *THINK* she's in any of my classes. I suppose I'd better ask someone.

Oh—someone's dropped an envelope.

And so—

Abbie? She's off with the flu just now. She lives near the Post Office, I think. Sorry, I've got to rush!

Oh—thanks.

I thought Sandra might be more helpful than the others, but she's not.

I'll deliver it after school . . . English next. I wonder if anyone will speak to me? I used to enjoy English at my old school, but here I dread everything!

After school—

Now, which way do I go?

Excuse me, which way is the Post Office?

Down the end of the road, left, right at the crossroads, right, then left.

55

Suddenly—

I saw you coming from the window. I've been so worried.

I found her wandering about, so I thought I'd better try and find her house.

I'm rushed off my feet at the moment. You see, my mum's ill, so I've *TWO* houses to keep. What Sarah really needs is a baby-sitter.

I know this is a bit forward of me, but, well—*YOU* wouldn't like to baby-sit occasionally, would you? Sarah's taken to you, I can see that. She's not usually very good with strangers.

I'd like to help if I can.

Come inside and I'll give you my phone number. When you've checked up with your parents, you can give me a ring.

Now, that's our phone number. Phone any night this week.

Yes, thank you, I will. I should go now, I've got a letter to deliver before tea— if you can give me directions, that is!

A short time later—

There's the Post Office now. That's strange, I seem to recognise this road—wait a minute—I live near here! I'd forgotten all about the Post Office being near my new house. How stupid!

Williams . . . this must be Abbie's house.

Just then—

Hi, can I help you? Hey—you're the new girl aren't you? Just come in. Mum's at the shops just now, and I'm not supposed to get up.

Right.

And so—

It's good to have some company. I've been stuck in here for ages.

I found this letter in the corridor at school. It's got your name on it, so I thought I'd deliver it.

That was nice of you . . . oh great, it's an invitation to Kate's party on Saturday. I should be better by then.

That's good.

It must be nice having a party to go to.

58

I know—you can come too. I'll phone Kate now and ask her. She won't mind, though. Then you'll be able to make friends with everyone. Let's go downstairs.

But, I . . .

But Abbie wouldn't listen—

So it's okay? Great. Yes . . . yes, I'll see you then—'bye!

Abbie's nice. I'm glad I met her.

Thanks, Abbie.

It's nothing. Hey, how about coming in for me on Saturday morning? You can come and help me choose an outfit. I'd better dash back to bed now. If Mum sees I'm up, she'll send me back to school! 'Bye!

That's great. I've made a friend at last—and I've a party to go to.

Back home—

Sorry I'm late, Mum. Mmmm, something smells good. I'm starving!

That's good to hear. You've done nothing but pick at your food for ages. You're looking a lot happier, too.

I am, Mum, I've had a great day.

And it's all thanks to a letter!

Next day—

Coming for lunch, Mel?

I'll join you in a minute, Sandra. I've something to do first.

That's that done. Now for lunch.

I'll leave it here. Someone else might be lonely like I was . . .

Melanie Edwards

THE END

MUM'S BARGAINS

SUSIE CARTER'S mum was always bringing home bargains—not all of them exactly useful! One day—

Just put it there, please. Susie, I'm home! Come and see what I've bought.

It's nice and quiet today—I wonder where Mum is? I hope she hasn't got herself another bargain!

Oh, dear—she has! I wonder what she's got THIS time.

No wonder! Oh, Mum, we can't keep this. For a start, where are we going to put it?

Oh! I'd—er—never thought of that . . . er . . . what are we going to do?

A gorilla?

Well, I was passing a theatrical shop, and there was a clearance sale on. The man let me have it for next to nothing—AND he delivered it personally!

We'll have to give it away—and I think I know where . . .

And so—

But do you think the Children's Home will *WANT* a stuffed gorilla, Susie?

Of course they will— kids love things like this . . .

But—

I don't think they like it, Susie. Still, it was a nice idea.

Sorry, Matron. I didn't realise it would scare them.

Oh, Gus. What *ARE* we going to do with you?

Well, I know what *I'M* doing—going home to get your tea on. Good luck!

I've got an idea, Gus! I know a place where you'll be wanted— come on!

And—

. . . so I thought you might want Gus for the Museum.

Mmm . . . would you come this way, please?

Crumbs! A room full of stuffed gorillas! So you won't be wanting Gus, then?

I'm afraid not. Oh, dear, people are *SO* generous, I hate to refuse—but you can see how it is.

We may as well go home—I'll think better with some food inside me . . . oh, there's Jane. Jane—hi! Meet Gus, our gorilla.

It's one of Mum's bargains. I'm taking it home.

I'm glad my mum's got nice quiet hobbies. All she does is hang-gliding and sword swallowing. Oh— here's the bus!

Look at him—imagine having a face like that. They should've left him in the jungle!

Ha! Ha!

Cheeky brats!

I didn't realise the conductor on that bus looked like Gus. Sorry, Jane. I've got YOU thrown off too!

It's okay, the next stop was mine anyway. I'll just walk. 'Bye, Susie.

You're nothing but a nuisance, you know that? Oh, you're heavy, I'll have to put you down for a minute.

What's that? Hey—I've had another idea.

THE JUNGLE LOOK IS IN!

And so, at last, Gus found a home!

THE JUNGLE LOOK IS IN!

He looks good there. I knew the window lacked something.

At least Gus feels wanted now. Wait till I tell Mum!

That was great, Susie. And you got more than I paid for him.

Yes. Actually, I think there's something we should do with the extra money.

And next day—

It was very nice of you to buy the children sweets, Mrs Carter.

I thought it would make up for the fright they got. Besides, you shouldn't thank me . . .

. . . you should thank Gus!

THE END

THE MEERLEY MYSTERY

LONG ago, when young Evie Granger was left an orphan she was thrown on to hard times—

I'm alone in the world now, Cousin Leonard, and I'm almost penniless. I shall have to earn my living.

I've always had to work for my keep, Evie. Oh—how I'd like to be rich!

A few weeks later—

My visit is to bring this, Evie. It seems to be just the situation for you.

I do hope the situation is still vacant—for I fear the little money I *DO* have will soon be gone.

WANTED
COMPANION FOR
YOUNG LADY
APPLY
MRS. MELTON
GRAY'S HOTEL

I'll go to see Mrs Melton at once. A companion needs no training and I may be suitable.

After a short interview at Gray's Hotel—

You will be ideal for the post, Miss Granger. My niece, Bella, is sure to like you.

I have the appointment? Oh—thank you!

Thanks to Leonard, I shall now have a home—and a living.

Before you meet Bella, there are special conditions attached to your duties. First, you must be known as Dory Dean.
If you say so, Mrs Melton. But may I ask why?
Certainly. Poor Bella was involved in an accident in which her former companion died. The girl's name was Dory Dean. Bella has never accepted the tragic truth, and thinks that Dory is still alive.
That's very sad. Of course I agree, if it will be of help to Bella.
Thank you. Also, please watch Bella carefully at all times, and don't leave her alone for very long. She is not strong in her mind.
I understand. I'll take great care of Bella.
Dory! I knew you'd come back to us.
Yes. I'm here, Bella.
The poor girl is living in her own little world. She actually believes I'm her friend who died.
We'll be very happy now. We must not stray far from the house again, Dory. It isn't safe.
We'll do whatever you want, Bella.
The accident has made her nervous and unsure. It will take time to re-build her confidence.

You see? It's lovely walking . . . Oh—who is this?

Let's go back, Dory! I'm scared.

Good day! I'm looking for a young lady who . . .

We can't help you. I'm Bella Melton and my friend is Dory Dean. We don't know anybody else.

That's right. I must take Bella back to the house. She hasn't been well.

I'm sorry to have troubled you, Miss.

Back at the house—

You should not have gone out. This upset is a great setback. Bella is afraid of strangers.

I know—and I'm sorry that it happened. But Bella is like a prisoner in her own house, Mrs Melton. I am only trying to help her.

That night—

That's strange—I hear Bella's voice—yet she went to bed hours ago—and I'm sure she was still in bed when I went to get a drink of water . . .

She's fast asleep! It's good to relax and be myself!

What does that mean? Bella looks and sounds quite different.

We didn't hear you, Dory! Er—Bella is perfectly all right.

I had a bad dream... I-I couldn't sleep!

I see. Well, goodnight.

They seemed troubled at seeing me—but why, unless they had something to hide?

At times, I'm certain that Bella is as well and confident as anybody else. It's as if she's only pretending to be nervous and ill. But why? It's a mystery, and I don't like it.

I think I must leave, for I fear there is something happening in this house that I don't want to get involved in.

71

There's Mrs Melton talking to someone . . . but wait . . .

I'm sure that was my cousin Leonard—and he was talking with Mrs Melton!

They've gone! Or—did I imagine it?

No . . . I definitely saw them . . . arguing as if they knew each other well. But Leonard has never met Mrs Melton! Oh dear—I seem to be surrounded by mysteries!

I shouldn't have left Bella, but I'll only stay here a moment. It's refreshing to be alone and free . . . I suppose the real Dory Dean rests here, poor soul. I'll ask the path sweeper.

'I'M NOT A BOY!'

THIRTEEN - YEAR - OLD Samantha Dean was a tomboy—

'KEEPER!

MINE!

You'd look even more like a boy then, Sam.

You idiot, Sam—you could have saved that easily. We've lost the game now!

Sorry, boys—it's this hair of mine, it keeps getting in my way. Mum won't let me get it cut, though.

I suppose I would, Derek.

I don't want to be a boy—but I don't see why they should be the only ones who get to play all the best games!

On her way home—

Excuse me, son—do you have the time?

No, sorry.

He . . . he thinks I *AM* a boy! *I'M NOT A BOY!* I like playing with them, but I don't want to *BE* one.

I suppose I would look like a boy if it weren't for my long hair—and I certainly act like one, I admit that. Maybe it's time I started trying to behave a little more like a girl!

Next day—

Be Ashford's
MAY QUEEN
ENTRANTS MUST BE 12-16
APPLICATIONS TO MR CLARK
MAYOR'S OFFICE by APRIL

'Ashford's May Queen' . . . I wonder—no, I couldn't—but why not? I'll have as good a chance as anyone once I've started acting, and looking, like a girl. That'll give everyone at school something to think about.

And at school—

Hey look, Sam's combing her hair! What's wrong, Sam—are you feeling okay?

It's not a crime is it? And what's more *I'M* going in for the 'Ashford May Queen' Competition.

So she's entering it too, is she? Well at least I know I've not got much competition. Ha! Ha!

At break—

Hey, Sam—coming for a game of football?

No thanks, Steve.

Haven't you heard, Steve? Our Sam's turning into a lady. Ladies don't play football!

I don't care *WHAT* they say. I'll show them.

On Saturday—

I'm looking for a nice dress. Nothing too flashy.

This'll take all the money I was saving for a new leather football. It'll be worth it, though—I hope.

I think you looked better in the first dress.

I think you're right.

This competition isn't going to be such a walk-over as I thought. Hmm . . . I wonder if there's something I could do . . .

Back home—

The assistant on the beauty counter said I had to clean my skin thoroughly each day—and I've got some eye-shadow to try out. I never realised that being pretty was so expensive!

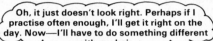

Oh, it just doesn't look right. Perhaps if I practise often enough, I'll get it right on the day. Now—I'll have to do something different with my hair.

This might not look too bad. I'll try it out at school, and see.

But—

What's happened, Sam? Get a fright, did you?

Hey look—it's the Ashford May Queen!

Rotten lot. I reckon they're right, though—this DOES look daft. Oh, who am I kidding? I'LL never be a beauty queen. It was a stupid idea in the first place.

No—why SHOULD I give up, because of them? I've never given up with anything before—and I'm not going to start now!

78

That night—

I've put conditioner on my hair, and a whole bottle of bubble bath in the bath. Poor mum doesn't know what's come over me! I must say I'm enjoying pampering myself like this. There's only two days till the competition, too—so I've not much time left.

On the day of the competition—

Ashford MAY QUEEN Competition TODAY!

I never thought I'd be nervous, but I am! Still, it'll all be over soon. Now, the competitors' room should be on the left here.

Here she comes now. My plan should see to it that she doesn't get anywhere.

I never thought there'd be so many people! Oh good—there's Louise from school.

Hi. Gosh, I'm glad I know someone. I'm so nervous I don't know how I'm going to get ready in time!

Hello, Sam. Don't worry—I'll help you.

And so—

I'm ready. Would you like me to make you up?

Oh, would you? I'd be really grateful.

I think I'll put your hair in a bun. I thought it was really nice when you wore it to school like that.

It looked awful, but it'll show *ME* up better.

Isn't there a mirror I could look in?

Later! There isn't time just now. Besides, I'm only putting on a touch of make-up. It makes all the difference.

And when Louise had finished—

You look great. We'd better dash now. The competition's beginning. Come on.

Okay.

I . . . oh no—look at me! Louise has done this deliberately. What a rotten thing to do! So *THAT'S* why she wouldn't let me look in a mirror. I'll have to do something quickly!

Now I've just to remove my make-up. I've no time to put any more on—but it'll have to do. And all the other girls look so pretty too. I haven't a chance.

By the end of the contest, Sam was feeling even more downhearted.

Oh well—back to jeans and football. I'll be a laughing stock after this.

. . . and the winner is—Samantha Dean! Well done, Samantha.

The judges decided on Samantha because of her natural fresh look.

I've won! And it was thanks to Louise, really.

And so, Sam the tomboy was the Ashford May Queen, with Louise as her attendant—

I made it! Goodbye, Sam the tomboy—hello, Samantha Dean, Beauty Queen!

Ashford May Queen

THE STABLE OF FAME

Over the ages, some of the most famous people in history have owed a great deal to their horses.

Alexander the Great, one of the great figures in Greek history, was aged thirteen when he was given BUCEPHALUS—a seemingly untameable black stallion. He broke and trained his horse without using harsh methods, and Alexander and his horse went on to win many great battles together.

The famous Byerley Arabian, Darley Arabian and Godolphin Barb were the original sires of all thoroughbred horses, and all racehorses can trace their ancestory back to them.

One of the most famous racehorses is Red Rum, who won the Grand National three times, and appeared on many guest shows, becoming a great celebrity, worldwide.

Valkyrie, a cheeky little black Shetland pony, was presented to Queen Elizabeth in 1960, by the people of the Shetland Isles, for Prince Andrew, and was a great favourite with the Royal children.

Another famous horse was Billy, the white police horse who controlled the vast crowds at Wembley Stadium in 1923, at the F.A. Cup Final between Bolton Wanderers and West Ham United.

81

CONTINUED ON PAGE 96.

My Favourite Place

THIS, I think, is my favourite spot. My very favourite. I come here quite often—I've always liked being on my own, you see. I like to sit on the rocks and watch the waves and listen to the wind, to think and to remember . . .

Yes, I'm alone often, but never lonely. At least, not until just lately . . .

" You shouldn't go up to The Point all by yourself," Sarah often cautions me—Sarah's my best friend.

" Those caves are dangerous when the tide's coming in or the sea's rough. Anyway, what would your mum say?"

" My mum'll never know," I always laugh. " Besides, it's not as if I'm a holiday-maker, is it? I was brought up here, remember? I'm used to the cliffs. I'm not stupid!"

" Well, why you want to go up there so much beats me." Sarah does go on! " Even the boys give that place a wide berth."

How could I ever make Sarah understand? The loneliness, the solitude... That's what I like about The Point. Ever since I was little, I've had to share a bedroom with our twins, Janet and Joy. It's only here at the sea edge that I can get any privacy to read or think. Nobody interrupts me here, you see.

Of course, like anyone else of my age, I love being with my friends as well. I love doing the usual things like going round the beach funfair, playing the pinball machines, hanging about the Promenade coffee bar. The sort of thing everyone round here does.

In fact, it was in that coffee bar that I first met Peter Tarrant.

Peter's really nice. Brown hair, friendly eyes and a great swimmer. He's won loads of silver cups for that. He's great fun to be with, too.

What's even better is that he likes me. At least, I think he does, because once he offered to teach me how to swim. That's the funny thing about me—I was born and bred by the sea, yet I've never been brave about going in the water. Actually, it's not really safe for proper bathing along this bit of coast, and the nearest public baths are about ten miles away, in Crampton-on-Sands.

So, what with one thing and another, I just haven't got around to learning to swim.

Peter was horrified when I confessed.

" Julie Trent! You ought to be ashamed of yourself," he told me with pretended sternness. Then he grinned. " Never mind. I'll show you how—we'll go over to Crampton sometime. Okay?"

So we arranged to meet each other at the coach station the next Saturday, to get the bus into Crampton. Somehow, though, we've never got around to those lessons yet . . . I can't really remember why . . .

I've got this strange feeling, though, that it's because of something that

happened not long ago . . . perhaps yesterday or the day before . . . I'm not sure . . . I can't remember it very clearly, it's all hazy in my mind. I do know that I came up here and it was a particularly wild night. I came to think about Peter, about our 'date' to go to Crampton, about what I would wear. I hugged my exciting new secret to myself. Oh, I was so happy . . .

The Point was deserted as usual. And I know I was silly, but I sat here and forgot everything . . . the time . . . the tide . . . everything . . .

To be truthful, when I think about that night now, all that comes back to me is the feeling of being wet . . . and cold, chilled right through . . . and terrified . . . the rest is a blur in my memory.

I only know I haven't seen Peter since then, or any of my friends. And I miss them so much . . . so very much . . .

Goodness! What's that? I think I can hear voices! Yes! That's Sarah's voice! And Peter's!

" Peter! Sarah!" I call out. " I'm here ! Over here . . . !"

Oh, great! I can see them now! Being alone is okay some of the time, but well, I need company sometimes, just like everyone else.

" Hi, there, you lot!" I call again, but my voice is thin, whipped away by the wind . . .

At last they're close, standing together on the opposite headland. Unsmiling, unhappy even . . .

Then Sarah speaks.

" That was her favourite place, I think. Over there. We told her it wasn't safe, but she wouldn't listen."

There's a funny catch in her throat, and even from here I can tell she's near to tears.

" I still can't take it in," Peter says to her. He shakes his head and his eyes are clouded.

" We shouldn't have come," Sarah goes on. " It's too soon . . . "

" Let's go, then," Peter says. " The wind's getting up and the tide's on the turn."

He turns to go—I can't believe it! They still haven't spotted me!

" Sarah!" I shout again as loudly as I can. And frantically, I wave. Surely she can see me, she's looking straight across, straight at me!

" Wait!" She runs after Peter and puts a hand on his arm. " Just a sec. Did you hear anything just then? A voice . . . someone calling my name . . . ?"

Peter stops in surprise and listens for a minute. Then he shrugs.

" You're imagining things, Sarah. It must be a bird calling, or the wind. Come on. It's no use hanging about here, it's too . . . too heartbreaking . . . "

" I know." Sarah wipes her eyes on her sleeve. " But I had to come, just to say ' goodbye '." She turns to face me.

" Goodbye, Julie!" Her voice has almost dropped to a whisper, but I know what she's saying.

They're going now—skipping hurriedly, but carefully, from rock to rock and over the foaming, tide-filled creeks .

They're going away from me . . . forgetting me. Sarah . . . ! Peter . . . ! Please come back!

" Just to say ' goodbye '." That's what Sarah said. " Goodbye." Why . . . ?

Then, suddenly, I know . . . Suddenly it all comes to me . . . It all begins to make sense . . . Sadness sweeps over me, overwhelms me, engulfs me . . .

" Sarah . . . ! Peter . : . ! Goodbye . . . !" I cry out. But my words are lost forever in the sound of the crashing waves . . .

Charmette

ONCE upon a time there was a trendy, fun-loving fairy called Charmette—

Betcha wish you could roller skate like me, huh? I'll let you into a little secret— it's my wings that give me the extra edge!

Oh-oh! I hear footsteps! Time to unbuckle my skates, and get back into the wish-granting business, again!

Smiley

PEGGY SHAW, affectionately called Smiley by the staff, was a long-term patient in the children's ward at St Martin's Hospital and took a helpful interest in the other patients.

Here's your elevenses, Sylvia. Hey, you're looking pretty pleased with yourself.

I feel it, Peggy! Sister's just told me I'm to have an X-ray this afternoon to check up on how my back is doing. If the results are good, I can say goodbye to my plaster—and I'll be able to start ice-skating again.

That's great news.

Sylvia is dead keen on ice skating, and she's good at it, from all accounts—won a lot of competitions. I hope she's given good news this afternoon.

But, that afternoon—

I'm very sorry, my dear. I know how hopeful you were, but these things can't be rushed.

It was bad news—that's obvious. Poor Sylvia!

89

The following morning, an item in the local newspaper caught Peggy's attention.

I wonder . . . it might work. It's worth a try, anyway. I'll ask Sister for permission to go out this afternoon, into the town. I've enough money to pay for a taxi there and back. It's worth it if my idea will help Sylvia.

As a long-term patient, and one with a reputation for being reliable, Peggy was allowed the occasional outing.

I wish I could have spared a nurse to go with you. Still, you've been out on your own before, and you're a sensible girl. Enjoy your treat, dear.

Thanks, Sister. I'll be back by around half-past four.

Sister thinks I'm treating myself to tea at the Park Hotel. Well, I AM going there, but not for tea. I want to see Miss Madison, it said in the paper she's a guest there this week. She is a very famous ice skater, a real star, and I hope she'll be kind and want to help Sylvia.

Later, at the hotel—

Checked out? B-but it said in the paper she'd be here until tomorrow.

A sudden change of plan, so Miss Madison told me. She left for the station . . . oh, about five minutes ago, to catch the three-fourteen train to London.

I wanted to tell her about Sylvia, to get her to write a letter to Sylvia, telling her to keep hoping. Sylvia is a great fan of Miss Madison's. But I won't give up! Perhaps I can get to the station in time.

At the station—

I'm too late! Oh, I wish I could move faster—this stupid leg of mine!

I've used up all my money. Shall I take a taxi? The hospital would pay for it, at the other end. No, I won't. Why should they pay out good money, just because my idea didn't work?

When Peggy reached the hospital—

Smiley! Thank goodness! Sister Mason has been so worried, and thinking of phoning the police. You look worn out!

Walked . . . from the station . . . Leg . . . tired . . .

She's fainted!

Later—

. . . and—and that was my idea, Sister, but it went wrong. I did so want to help Sylvia! I'm sorry I've caused so much trouble.

Don't cry, Peggy. That warm heart of yours might win the day after all. Now, off to sleep with you.

The next morning—

Oh Peggy, I'm so ashamed of myself. Sister has told me how hard you tried to help me. But what you did, Peggy—it's not wasted. I've decided to stop brooding and feeling sorry for myself, to be hopeful—and to have faith in the doctors. Thanks, Peg!

My idea didn't work out as planned, but it HAS worked—and that's what counts!

THE END

"I AM Margaret!"

TWELVE-YEAR-OLD Margaret Soames got on well with her family—Mum, Dad and Jimmy, who was ten. But, truth to tell, Margaret was sometimes a little thoughtless and selfish. But people who only think of themselves usually get punished in some way. This is what happened to Margaret—

'Bye then—I'm off to meet Janie. We're going for a wander.

Be back in time for tea then.

I'm going to the park to play football.

Careful in the traffic, Jim.

Hi, Janie.

The girls set off, chattering all the way—

. . . so I had to do the dishes myself, even though it made me late for the Guides.

I hate doing dishes. I get out of it quite often by pretending I don't feel well. You should try it.

Hello, Margaret. Shall we go down to Dale's Hollow? There should be lots of bluebells there just now—we could collect some for our nature study class.

92

95

ABOUT HORSES

Horses in MYTH LEGEND & FOLKLORE

Throughout the centuries, the horse has featured strongly in mythology. In Greek mythology, horses drew Apollo the sun god's chariot, and carried Poseidon, the sea god. Pegasus the sparkling, white, winged horse is even now a well known figure in their tales.

The colourful, Indian sun god—Indra—had a flaming chariot drawn by wild, mighty horses.

The Scottish poet, Robert Burns, included a horse in one of his most famous poems, "Tam O' Shanter". This was Meg, Tam's old mare, who saved him from the clutches of the local witches.

Another horse with very strange powers is " THE HARDY HORSE "—and you can read all about him on the opposite page!

99

Later—

Oh, Jill, where have you been? I've been so worried!

I had to rescue this gentleman from Hound Hill Cave, Mum!

My husband will be home soon. He'll drive you to hospital, Mr Hardy.

My leg's not that bad—thanks to your daughter. I must say I like your place here!

When Jill's father came home.

I'm very fond of these moors—even if I do get trapped in caves! Do you think I might buy a partnership in your farm and riding stables to give me a local interest in my retirement?

That's an interesting proposition, Mr Hardy.

So, later—

Never mind the customers you lost today, Jill! Mr Hardy is going to put money into our business, so now we'll be able to get our farm and stables all done up!

That's great news, Dad.

Look, Mr Hardy! The black horse . . . it's fading away . . . like a ghost!

See what I mean about our Hardy horse now, young lady? It certainly came to my rescue . . . and helped out your family, too!

THE END

101

I HATE BOYS WHO...

Say they'll come to visit... ...so YOU can do their homework!

Buy you an Easter Egg of plain chocolate...

...'cos they know you don't like plain chocolate!

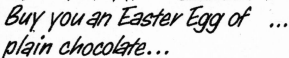

... come round to visit...

...after football practice!

Ask you out for the day...

...so you can look after their little cousin!

Come round for the evening...

...and spend it with your little brother!

Compliment you on your cooking...

...then try to feed it to your dog!

Becky! Look out!

Whoah!

AAAGH!

It's a child! Quickly—we must take her home and call a doctor!

R. Jones Ltd.

Later—

What happened? Wh . . . where am I?

Hush dear. I am Mrs Lyons. You must rest. You have had an accident.

It was then that Becky learned the dreadful truth.

Your injuries are serious, my dear. I am afraid you may never walk again. Only time will tell.

Never? Ohhh!

If I can't work, the orphanage will throw me out. I'll . . . I'll die in the gutter!

No, Becky. After the accident a stallholder told us who you were and we contacted the orphanage. You may stay with us.

The days passed and Becky became used to the idea of never walking again and settled down well with the Lyons.

Although I have no feeling in my legs, I'm happy here. Everything is so pretty and cheerful.

It was one morning in the garden that Becky made a startling discovery.

My . . . my legs are tingling. I have some feeling in them!

Dare I hope? Maybe someday I'll walk again!

What are you thinking, Becky, dear?

N . . . nothing, I was just day-dreaming.

With each passing day Becky felt her legs growing stronger until one day in her room—

I . . I can stand!

I can walk—*I CAN WALK!* I must tell Mr and Mrs Lyons!

The sudden movement frightened the kitten.

Oh! Snowy, come down, Snowy! I didn't mean to frighten you.

Snowy's stuck. She might fall and hurt herself. I will have to climb up and get her.

That stupid girl has left Becky. I will go and see if she is all right.

Oh, no! Mrs Lyons is coming. There isn't time to climb back down the tree!

I'll have to jump!

I'll have to make it seem as though I have fallen out of my chair.

BECKY! Are you all right? What happened?

Just in time! Now to look upset.

I . . . I thought Snowy was going up the tree. I leaned out of my chair to stop him and fell over. Dear Mrs Lyons, I did not mean to cause you trouble.

Dear child, if . . . if you can find it in your heart, Mr Lyons and I would be so glad if you would call us Mama and Papa.

I heard you call. Is anything wrong?

Becky had a fall but she says she is all right.

Still, I think you should lie down, Becky dear. I will make you a soothing cup of hot milk.

Thank you. You're too kind—both of you!

I have my own Mama and Papa now. I'm so glad I did not tell them I could walk, although I hate deceiving them this way.

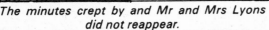

The minutes crept by and Mr and Mrs Lyons did not reappear.

Mama, Papa? Where are you? May I have my milk?

Smoke! And I smell burning! *MAMA! PAPA!*

Something dreadful is happening. Smoke is pouring from the kitchen!

Forgetting her secret, Becky rushed into the kitchen.

The smoke is overpowering! Mama and Papa have been overcome by it. I must get them out!

Must . . . get them out . . . into . . . garden!

I've got Mama out—but Papa is so much heavier.

Oh, no—Snowy! She's still inside!

Just then—

AAAGH! My back!

Moments later, Mr Lyons regained consciousness—

My Becky! She's still inside!

Don't worry, sir. We'll get her out.

I don't know whether the girl is alive or dead. Let's get her out of here!

It was some hours later when Becky awoke in her own room

Becky dear. It is your Mama.

I . . . I remember a fire . . .

Only the kitchen was badly damaged. We must have been rescued by passers-by. You too, Becky. Neither Papa nor I can remember much about it!

Then they do not realise I saved them. My secret is safe!

I'm afraid your spine was damaged when the timbers fell on you, Becky. The only consolation is that you were already used to your life in a wheelchair.

Mama, if . . . if I could have walked soon after you took me in, would . . . would you have sent me back to the Orphanage?

Never, my child. After a day, we knew you were to be the daughter we could never have. It would have only increased our joy had you regained the use of your legs.

All this time I have been deceiving these wonderful people for nothing. I could have walked and shared my happiness with them. Now that chance has gone—forever. *I'LL NEVER WALK AGAIN!*

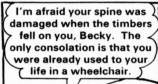

The doctor had not allowed for the advance of medical science, however. Five years later, a new operation enabled Becky to walk again. And, as her parents grew older, Becky was happy to care for them, and repay the loving kindness the Lyons had shown her. Fate had finally relented, and decided that Becky had paid the price of her strange deception . . .

THE END

ANGELA HAMILTON lived in London in Victorian times, and was the only child of a wealthy banker. When she was fourteen, Angela was stricken by an illness for which there was no known cure, and given only a year to live. Wishing to put a quick end to her loving parents' distress, Angela faked her own death, then went to one of the poorest areas of London, determined to devote her remaining time to helping the city's many needy waifs.

Angela rented a large stable to provide shelter for as many of the waifs as it would house. One afternoon—

Home is a welcome sight on such a cold day, is it not, Annie?

That it is, Miss Angel, though the cold don't bother me like it used to, now I've got decent clothes, an' boots, an' good food inside me.

Them things is ever so nice, but what makes me happiest of all is that you loves me, hump back an' all. It's ever so good to be loved, isn't it, Miss Angel?

Indeed it is, Annie.

Here she is! We was gettin' worried about you, Miss Angel.

The shopping took much longer than usual, children. With Christmas coming, the market was very crowded.

I've set the table for tea, Miss Angel, and put the kettle on to boil.

I've kept the fire going, Miss Angel. Just as well, too, 'cos your hands are frozen.

But my heart is glowing, with the warmth of their welcome.

Matt, has Luke been sitting there on his own all afternoon?

Yes, Miss Angel. I told him he was welcome to sit by the fire with the rest of us, but he just scowled at me. He's a sour 'un, is Luke.

Life has soured him, Matt, and small wonder. As you know, he was abandoned by his uncaring parents when he was but four years old, and has fended for himself ever since. He has never known love.

But that's all changed now, Miss Angel. You've given him a home and you wants to give him love, too.

Yes, Matt, but he is not yet ready to accept it.

The broken ribs which Luke sustained when those bully boys set upon him are healing well. But the deeper scars, in his heart, will not be so easily healed.

After tea—

It's a cold night, Luke. You would be warmer sitting by the fire.

I'm all right where I am.

115

Give me that piece of string and . . .

No! It's mine! I found it afore I came here. I didn't steal it off you.

I was not suggesting that you had. I just wanted to show you something with your string. It can be made into what is called a Cat's Cradle. I thought it might amuse you.

I ain't interested. It's MY string. I don't want to be amused.

Very well. Luke, tomorrow is Christmas Eve and some of the boys are going out to gather holly. Would you like to go with them?

No, but if you thinks it's time I was earning my keep, then I will.

The holly will not be sold, but used to decorate the stable-house for Christmas. I just thought the expedition would be fun for you. You do not HAVE to earn your keep, Luke.

What's the catch?

There is no catch. I care about you, Luke. This is your home. Your keep is given to you willingly.

There must be a catch in it somewhere.

He is as prickly as holly, and so unhappy. He never smiles. Poor, poor Luke! I wish I could do more to help him.

That night, as usual, Angela took food to the hungry waifs she was unable to house.

It was here, almost two weeks ago, that I came across Luke, so dreadfully thin and his eyes filled with pain and hopelessness. My heart went out to him then, and it aches for him now.

But his heart is closed, locked against a world which has treated him so cruelly. If he is to be happy, the doors of his heart must be opened to let in love.

Love is the source of faith and hope, and of the strength to face hardship bravely and without bitterness. The only true and lasting happiness comes from the giving and receiving of love!

I'll come again tomorrow, and earlier than usual as it will be Christmas Eve. Goodnight, children. God bless you.

He has blessed us, 'cos Miss Angel cares about us.

Angela made her way to Hobbs Court, where a little girl was gravely ill with pneumonia.

Doctor John is devoting all his skills towards saving little Sarah's life. Day and night he is at her bedside. He must be tired. Perhaps I can persuade him to take a rest while I watch over her.

I am so glad that I befriended him when, because of one fatal error of judgement, he had lost faith in himself, and become a drifter. At times I despaired of ever restoring his confidence, but it came about at last and now he helps me with my work.

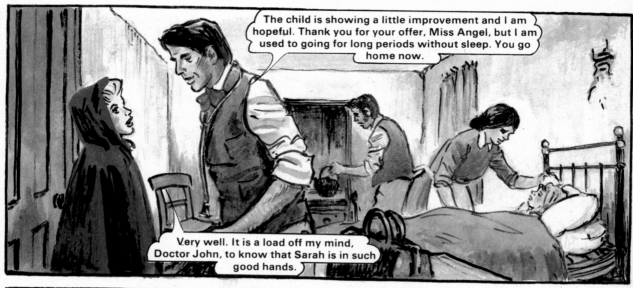

The child is showing a little improvement and I am hopeful. Thank you for your offer, Miss Angel, but I am used to going for long periods without sleep. You go home now.

Very well. It is a load off my mind, Doctor John, to know that Sarah is in such good hands.

I am glad to hear that, for Angela has more than enough loads to carry. What a fine girl she is. Her courage, her giving, loving nature, is a bright light in an often dark world.

I promised Annie that I would go to bed as soon as I had drunk my tea, but I am so tired, so very, very tired, that it will take a big effort to get to my feet.

My physical strength fades a little more with each day, and often my body is racked with pain. How good it would be to feel Mama's loving arms about me, to see her dear face, and my Papa's . . .

But this will not do! There is so much work to be done— and so little time left to me. I must not waste one moment in self-pity, or on selfish thoughts.

My spirit must burn strong and help me to hold out for as long as possible, for the sake of my dear, precious waifs.

The following evening—

I've put your chair closest to the fire, Miss Angel.

Can we stay up later than usual tonight, Miss Angel, 'cos it's Christmas Eve, like?

Yes, you may. How good it is to be home, for it is snowing heavily now.

You didn't eat much dinner, Miss Angel, so I've put the last of the broth on to heat for you. When it's ready you're to drink every drop, else I'll be *VERY* cross with you.

All right, Annie. I promise I'll be good.

Tell us a story, please, Miss Angel.

Ooh, yes!

Very well, children. I'll tell you the story of the first Christmas, when Jesus was born.

God chose Mary to be the mother of Jesus, and Joseph, who was a carpenter, to be his foster father—that is, to take care of Jesus till he grew up.

Why didn't God choose a rich toff what could give Jesus more?

God didn't want Jesus to grow up in a big house, or a palace, away from ordinary people. And Joseph was a very good and kind man.

Oh.

Angela told how Herod, the King of Judea, had ordered all his subjects to return to the town of their birth, to be counted. Mary and Joseph had both been born in Bethlehem.

So Mary and Joseph travelled there from their home in Nazareth. After they had been counted, they could not return home at once, for Jesus was soon to be born. They needed shelter, and there was no room at the inn.

But the innkeeper took pity on them and let them sleep in his stable. And there the little Baby Jesus was born.

In a stable! Ooh!

Angela related how an angel of the Lord told some shepherds the glad tidings, and how they made their way to the stable to see Baby Jesus.

And then came Three Wise Men, who had travelled from afar, guided by a bright star. They were rich, important men, but they knelt before Baby Jesus, and gave him precious gifts—gold, and frankincense and myrrh. Being so wise, they knew he was the Son of God.

And that, children, is the story of our Lord Jesus, born in a lowly stable, but surrounded by love.

Just then, there was a faint knock at the door.

I'm sorry to trouble you, but I'm at my wits' end. Are you the Miss Angel we've heard of, who helps those in need?

Yes—what can I do for you?

My name is John Smith and this is my wife, Martha. Martha's baby is due very soon and we can't find anywhere to spend the night. Everywhere is full up.

We could go to the workhouse, but—oh, Miss! It would break my heart to have our child born there!

I understand. Come inside. You are very welcome.

God bless you, Miss.

Thank you, Miss.

Come and sit by the fire.

I'll put some more wood on.

You must be chilled to the bone.

Now let's have these wet boots off, Mrs Martha.

This broth will do her good. Her need is greater than mine.

You don't sound like a Londoner, mister.

We came here only six months ago. I thought I could earn better money in London, but it hasn't worked out. We're country folk, and haven't taken to city life.

When Martha is well enough to travel, we'll go back to the village in Sussex where we grew up and where we wed, eh, Martha?

Yes, John.

I can see that they are good folk and that there is deep love between them.

When Martha had finished the broth, and her husband the bread and cheese which Angela provided—

Here's your nightdress, Mrs Martha. I've put a brick on to heat, Miss Angel. It'll warm the bed.

I don't like to take your bed, Miss Angel.

But you must. You are welcome to it.

When Mrs Smith was in bed—

Let me go and fetch Doctor John. It's snowing hard, Miss Angel.

It is best that I go, Matt, for if Doctor John is unable to leave Sarah, I shall have to go in search of another doctor.

Walk on nails, Miss Angel would, if it would help someone in need. She never spares herself. She's a real angel right here on Earth!

My legs are tiring, but I must keep going. Not much further now. Oh! I do hope Doctor John will be able to tend Mrs Smith.

He has so much skill, and such a good heart. I want a kind person to bring Martha and John's first born child into the world.

All was well. Sarah's fever had broken and she could safely be left in her mother's care.

I had to sell Sarah's baby clothes when times was extra hard, but I couldn't bring myself to part with this shawl. Now I want it to be put to good use in gratitude for my child being spared. Take it for the new baby, Miss Angel.

Thank you, Mrs Tulley.

Later—

Mister I been thinking that your baby will be special, 'cos of being born at Christmas, same as Jesus. That'll be nice for 'im.

He—or she—will be very special to my wife and me, son, that's for sure.

ALL babies, ALL children, are special, Bobby, in their own way. You are very special to me—very precious.

Thank you, Miss Angel!

Just then—

There's the church clock, striking the hour, Miss Angel.

The hour of midnight. It's almost Christmas Day.

A moment later there came another sound—

The baby! Its first cry! The child is born!

Mr Smith, your wife is safely delivered of a baby daughter.

Praise be to the Lord!

Listen! Listen to the church bells! Isn't it a happy sound, Miss Angel?

Happy and triumphant—for they ring out the Christmas message of new life, and new hope!

Don't the stars look bright, Miss Angel? I reckons they're shining extra bright tonight, for our little Christmas baby, born in a stable.

And surrounded by love!

A little later, the children were allowed to see the baby.

Oh, the little love! I ain't never seen a prettier baby!

Nor me!

The waifs each found a small gift for the baby.

Thank you, children!

My dear waifs! Each of them is giving something he or she holds precious.

Only Luke hangs back. What is in his mind, his heart, I do not know, but I shall not give up hope.

Angela waited, and then—

It's just like the story Miss Angel told us.

Very slowly, Luke approached the bed, and laid his piece of string beside the other presents.

For the baby.

It's all I've got.

Then it *IS* treasure, Luke—more valuable than gold, or frankincense or myrrh.

Aye! Thank you, Luke. It is indeed a treasured gift!

He is smiling! And it is a smile of *HOPE!*

I prayed last night for a miracle for Luke, and I believe that Martha and her husband were guided to the stable-house.

Miss Angel, you've been so kind to us and, if you're willing, we'd like to name our baby Angela, after you.

Oh, yes! I would like that very much. Please, may I hold her for a moment?

Little Angel, I hope you will be blessed with the great gift of good health. But, even more important, I hope you will be blessed with a caring nature, and a warm and loving heart— for then you will know true happiness!

The End

HOW SUPERSTITIOUS ARE YOU?

The truth is about to be revealed! Are you VERY superstitious, only slightly superstitious—or do you think superstitions are all a lot of nonsense? Are you the type of person who doesn't sing before breakfast, cut her nails on a Sunday, or dare to look at a new moon through a window? Do you rush to touch wood every time you tempt fate—or couldn't you care less?

Here's a quiz specially for "Mandy" readers to help you find out just how superstitious YOU are.

1. You're clearing the table after dinner and accidentally knock the salt over. Do you:—
   A) Gasp in horror and quickly throw a pinch over your left shoulder?
   B) Say "Oh dear, isn't that supposed to be unlucky?" then carry on clearing the table?
   C) Brush the salt on to the floor while no one's looking?

2. Your mum's been nagging you about the state of your room again, so you devote a whole Saturday to clearing it out. You're almost finished when 'CRACK' you stand on your hand mirror which has somehow found its way on to the floor and smash it to bits. Do you:-
   A) Put on all the lucky charms you can find and stay indoors for the next seven years?
   B) Hope your mum doesn't find out—or you WILL be in for some bad luck?
   C) Collect the bits together and chuck them out—you didn't like it much anyway?

3. You're queueing up to see the ballet and you drop one of your gloves in a puddle. Do you:—
   A) Leave it where it is?
   B) Hope that someone will pick it up for you?
   C) Pick it up and wring it out?

4. You and your family are out for a picnic one Sunday afternoon and you find a four-leafed clover. Do you:—
   A) Pick it, take it home and press it carefully, for luck?
   B) Leave it—you don't like picking growing things, but feel pleased that you've been lucky enough to find one?
   C) Grab it up with a handful of grass and stuff it all down your brother's shirt because he's been annoying you all day?

126